D0821742

CALGARY PUBLIC LIBRARY

MAY - 2012

Author:

Jacqueline Morley studied English at Oxford University, England. She has taught English and history, and now works as a freelance writer. She has written historical fiction and nonfiction for children, including several books on ancient Egypt.

Artist:

David Antram was born in Brighton, England, in 1958. He studied at Eastbourne College of Art and then worked in advertising for 15 years before becoming a full-time artist. He has illustrated many children's nonfiction books.

Series creator:

David Salariya was born in Dundee, Scotland. He has illustrated a wide range of books and has created and designed many new series for publishers in the UK and overseas. David established The Salariya Book Company in 1989. He lives in Brighton with his wife, illustrator Shirley Willis, and their son, Jonathan.

Editors: **Karen Smith, Stephen Haynes**

Editorial Assistant: **Mark Williams**

PAPER FROM SUSTAINABLE FORESTS

© The Salariya Book Company Ltd MMXII

No part of this publication may be reproduced in whole or in part, or stored in a retrieval system, or transmitted in any form or by any means, electronic, mechanical, photocopying, recording, or otherwise, without written permission of the publisher. For information regarding permission, write to the copyright holder.

This edition published in Great Britain in 2012 by
The Salariya Book Company Ltd
25 Marlborough Place, Brighton BN1 1UB

ISBN-13: 978-0-531-20874-8 (lib. bdg.) 978-0-531-20949-3 (pbk.)
ISBN-10: 0-531-20874-5 (lib. bdg.) 0-531-20949-0 (pbk.)

All rights reserved.
Published in 2012 in the United States
by Franklin Watts
An imprint of Scholastic Inc.
Published simultaneously in Canada.

A CIP catalog record for this book is available
from the Library of Congress.

Printed and bound in China.
Printed on paper from sustainable sources.
1 2 3 4 5 6 7 8 9 10 R 21 20 19 18 17 16 15 14 13 12

SCHOLASTIC, FRANKLIN WATTS, and associated logos are trademarks and/or registered trademarks of Scholastic Inc.

This book is sold subject to the conditions that it shall not, by way of trade or otherwise, be lent, resold, hired out, or otherwise circulated without the publisher's prior consent in any form or binding or cover other than that in which it is published and without similar condition being imposed on the subsequent purchaser.

The mummy's curse! A gripping tale... but is it true?

You Wouldn't Want to Be
Cursed by King Tut!

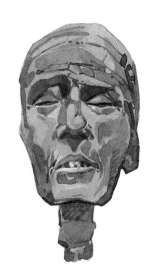

Written by
Jacqueline Morley

Illustrated by
David Antram

Created and designed by
David Salariya

A Mysterious Death You'd Rather Avoid

Franklin Watts®
An Imprint of Scholastic Inc.
NEW YORK • TORONTO • LONDON • AUCKLAND • SYDNEY
MEXICO CITY • NEW DELHI • HONG KONG
DANBURY, CONNECTICUT

Contents

Introduction   5

The Boy King   7

The King Must Live Forever   8

To the Land of the Dead   10

A Borrowed Tomb?   12

Intruders!   14

The Valley of the Kings   16

Making Headlines   18

Lord Carnarvon Dies   20

The Fate of a Canary   22

The Rumors Grow   24

The Death Toll Rises   26

The Real Victim   28

Glossary   30

Index   32

Introduction

t's 1922, and the newspaper that you work for—the *Times*, based in London, England—is sending you to cover the greatest story of your career. A short time ago, two Englishmen uncovered a flight of steps leading to the burial place of an ancient Egyptian king, or *pharaoh*. They broke through a sealed door and found the body of the king, surrounded by immense treasure, lying in a solid gold coffin. He had lain undisturbed for over three thousand years.

Those two Englishmen are Lord Carnarvon, a rich aristocrat eager to find ancient Egyptian remains; and Howard Carter, the archeologist he has hired to help him. Their discovery is making newspaper headlines worldwide. Many readers are fascinated by the exotic-looking gods and mysterious writing of ancient Egypt.

But a series of very unexpected events is about to unfold—and there is talk of an ancient curse on anyone who disturbs the pharaoh. Could this be true?

You're eager to find out more about the boy king—but you definitely wouldn't want to be cursed by him!

A statue of a pharaoh's ka *(spirit)*

The Boy King

The pharaoh whose tomb has just been discovered was called Tutankhamen.* Very little is known about his reign, but it was short and probably not very happy. He became king when he was only nine, at a time when things were not going well in Egypt. His father, Akhenaten, had upset people by forcing them to worship a new god. When Akhenaten died, many officials saw a chance to undo his work by having power over the new boy king, who was too young to rule without help. The new king's advisers wanted him to do what they wanted. Poor Tutankhamen must have wondered if he could trust anyone.

Also spelled Tutankhamun

HUNTING in the desert was a royal pastime that the young king may have enjoyed.

TUTANKHAMEN was married to his half sister. This was quite common; pharaohs often married their sisters.

HE WAS ONLY 18 when he died, in 1323 BC. No one knows whether it was because of an illness, an accident, or something sinister.

7

The King Must Live Forever

The boy king Tutankhamen had to do more than rule—he also had to play the part of a god. His people believed that each of their pharaohs was the son of the sun god, Ra. Through this relationship, Egyptians enjoyed the special favor of the gods. Upon his death, each pharaoh was reunited with the sun god, ensuring that Egypt would continue to receive the gods' blessings. This could not happen if the pharaoh's body decayed, as his spirit would perish with it—a dreadful fate that all Egyptians tried to avoid by having their bodies mummified. In the case of a pharaoh, this was done with the utmost care, with an attending priest acting the role of the embalmer-god, Anubis.

Anubis mask

Stop mumbling! Read the spells clearly.

Beetle

AMULETS: These charms were tucked in among the linen wrappings of the mummy to protect the dead pharaoh's spirit. A beetle with open wings, an oval scarab beetle, and an eye were all emblems of the sun god.

Eye of Ra

8

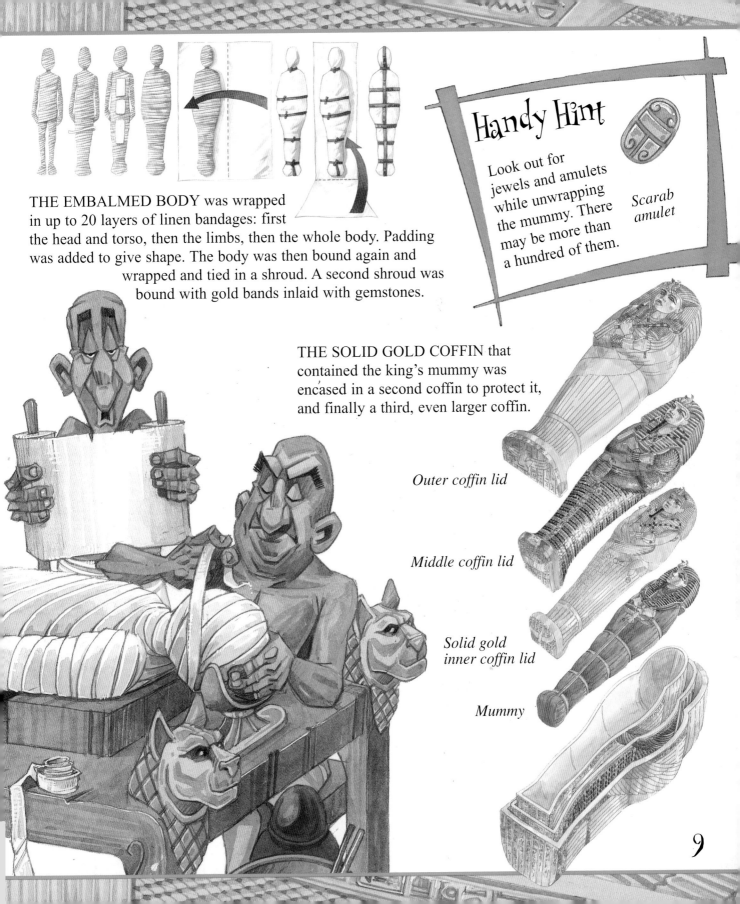

THE EMBALMED BODY was wrapped in up to 20 layers of linen bandages: first the head and torso, then the limbs, then the whole body. Padding was added to give shape. The body was then bound again and wrapped and tied in a shroud. A second shroud was bound with gold bands inlaid with gemstones.

Handy Hint

Look out for jewels and amulets while unwrapping the mummy. There may be more than a hundred of them.

Scarab amulet

THE SOLID GOLD COFFIN that contained the king's mummy was encased in a second coffin to protect it, and finally a third, even larger coffin.

Outer coffin lid

Middle coffin lid

Solid gold inner coffin lid

Mummy

9

To the Land of the Dead

A great procession of priests, courtiers, and mourners brought Tutankhamen's coffin to his tomb.

THE LAND OF THE DEAD lay in the west, so Tutankhamen's tomb was in the western hills. His body was carried across the River Nile from the land of the living on the east bank.

THE TOMB was cut into the slopes of a hidden valley where many pharaohs lay buried. In modern times, the area has been named the Valley of the Kings.

Behind the coffin walked servants bearing goods to be stored in the tomb. They carried food of all types, clothes, furniture, chariots, weapons, model boats, small figures of people (to serve the pharaoh in the afterlife), and caskets full of fabulous jewelry. These items were for the pharaoh to use in the land of the dead. It may seem like a magnificent send-off for a pharaoh who hadn't reigned long or done much, but the most famous pharaohs were probably buried with far greater riches. We can't be sure, because their tombs were plundered long ago.

Handy Hint

The Valley of the Kings is one of the most important historical sites in the world. Make sure to dig there to make great discoveries.

R. Nile

BEFORE BURIAL, the ceremony of the Opening of the Mouth was held. The new pharaoh, who was also chief priest, touched the mummy with ritual tools. This restored the use of the king's senses in the afterlife.

Now he's looking a lot more lively!

11

A Borrowed Tomb?

The ancient Egyptians believed that an undisturbed tomb was a guarantee of immortality. While the body lay in the tomb, preserved and protected, its spirit would not perish. Most pharaohs ordered that large tombs be prepared for them well in advance.

Tutankhamen, however, was buried in a tomb so small that there was almost no room for his "baggage" for the next world. Perhaps his death was so unexpected that there was no tomb ready and he was placed in someone else's. His mummy, in its three coffins, was set in a magnificent stone sarcophagus covered by four gilded shrines. Then priests swept away all traces of footprints from the floor, and the tomb was sealed forever—or so they thought.

Rest in Peace?

THE GRAVE GOODS were carried down 16 steps, along a sloping passage, and into four rooms carved out of solid rock. After the funeral, all doors except the one to the most distant room were sealed.

THE JACKAL FIGURE of the god Anubis, preserver of the dead, kept eternal watch over the shrines that held the pharaoh's body.

13

Intruders!

Egyptians knew their pharaohs were buried with lots of treasure, and some people were ready to risk the anger of the gods to get it. But there is no record of a thief being struck down by a curse as a result. Many royal tombs were designed to foil thieves. Some had false turns and dangerous pits—but robbers still got in. Perhaps the tomb builders themselves were the robbers—they knew their way around!

Tutankhamen's tomb was broken into and resealed twice not long after his death. The thieves threw things around and got away with lots of jewelry. But later the tomb entrance was accidentally buried by rubble, and the robberies stopped.

AFTER THE TOMB WAS SEALED, the fresh plaster of the blocked-up doorways was stamped with seals like this. Its hieroglyphs call for the gods' protection over the tomb—but it's not a curse.

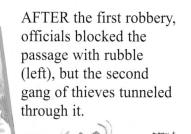

AFTER the first robbery, officials blocked the passage with rubble (left), but the second gang of thieves tunneled through it.

OFFICIALS who cleaned up after the robberies did just a quick job. Lots of items were put back in the wrong place.

ROBBERS may have been caught red-handed, because a bundle of valuable rings had been dropped, probably in their hurry to escape.

The Valley of the Kings

It was not until the 1700s that people realized the Valley of the Kings was the pharaohs' burial place. Then treasure hunters, and later archeologists, swarmed in. By the 1900s, many think there is little left to discover. But archeologist Howard Carter disagrees. He has a hunch that a little-known pharaoh, whose name is on a cup that has been dug up here, must be buried nearby. In November 1922 he finds some steps and unblocks a passage. Lord Carnarvon, Carnarvon's daughter, and his colleague Arthur Callender wait breathlessly as Carter peers through the passage.

IN THE EARLY 1800s, adventurer and showman Giovanni Belzoni made many finds in the valley. Scientific archeology developed later.

November 26, 1922

16

LORD CARNARVON is in poor health. He has had trouble breathing ever since he was seriously injured in a car crash. He came to Egypt to avoid damp English winters and took up excavating to pass the time.

Handy Hint

Don't forget that the smallest clue could lead to an exciting new discovery. This is the pottery cup that brought Howard Carter to the pharaoh's tomb.

YES! Wonderful things!

Making Headlines

The discovery is a world sensation. Never before has anyone found an Egyptian tomb still packed with almost all its contents. The site is immediately overrun by reporters, photographers, and sightseers hoping to get a glimpse of the incredibly rare objects as they are brought into the daylight. This is a slow process. There are thousands of objects in the tomb and Carter realizes that cataloging and removing each one carefully will take him years.

Meanwhile, reporters annoy the archeologists so much that Carnarvon decides to deal with just one newspaper. Luckily for you, it's the *Times*. All news about the finds is given only to your paper. But other reporters remain there in the hot Egyptian sun, irritated at being ignored. Some are tempted to "create" news stories for their papers, relying on rumors and guesswork.

It looks divine! But would it be comfortable?

IGNORING THE FUSS, Carter toils busily inside the tomb. Each object is photographed and carefully wrapped before removal to Cairo Museum.

18

Ritual bed in the shape of the cow goddess Mehit-Weret

THE TELEGRAPH OFFICE is overwhelmed by reporters who compete desperately to send their story before their rivals do.

LOCAL HOTELS run out of rooms and have to put up tents on the grounds to accommodate more people.

ARTHUR WEIGALL, a reporter from the London *Daily Mail*, once worked with Carter, so he is upset when he doesn't get special treatment. He needs news, so he encourages rumors. Weigall becomes among those who promote the idea of King Tut's curse.

Lord Carnarvon Dies

ess than two months later Lord Carnarvon is dead from an infected mosquito bite. Some reports hint that he was bitten while in the tomb. By now the tomb itself is old news, but readers lap up the new story of the unexpected death. Reports hint about strange omens and a curse. Letters to newspapers claim that the priests of ancient Egypt possessed mystic powers. In reality, however, there is no mystery about the death at all.

Did something just bite me?

ZZZZZZ

The Simple Truth

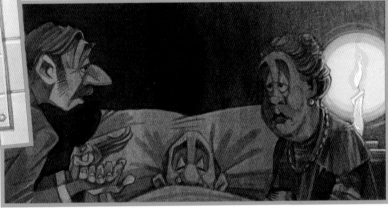

PNEUMONIA sets in. Already weak-lunged, Carnarvon dies in a Cairo hospital at 2:00 a.m. on April 5, 1923.

CARNARVON accidentally scrapes the scab off the mosquito bite while shaving. It becomes infected and causes blood poisoning.

Omens—or Coincidences?

AS CARNARVON'S WIFE AND SON close his eyes, an electrical blackout occurs. (But Cairo's electricity supply is known to be unreliable anyway!)

AT THAT VERY MOMENT, back in England, Carnarvon's dog, Susie, howls and dies! (But who really knows what time she died? Was anyone up at night to notice when she died, and did anyone account for the time difference between Egypt and England?)

21

The Fate of a Canary

More strange stories follow. It's reported that, sometime around the discovery of the steps leading to the tomb, Howard Carter's pet canary was eaten by a cobra. If that happened, no one noticed it at the time. But later, when the press starts its "curse of the pharaoh" campaign, the story becomes big news. According to Arthur Weigall, local people hired by Carter to dig at the site are sure this is Tutankhamen's vengeance on the person who disturbed his tomb. After all, the cobra goddess, Wadjit, appears on the pharaoh's headdress, rearing up to spit fire on his enemies.

Various versions of the canary story circulated, including these two:

1. AS SOON as the steps were found, Carter rushed to send a telegram to Carnarvon. As Carter entered his tent he saw a cobra eating his canary.

2. ONE DAY an assistant was sent by Carter to get something from his house. He found a coiled cobra in the canary cage!

COULD A SNAKE as big as a cobra really squeeze through the bars of a canary cage? *Yes!* In the 1990s, a TV team making a program about the tomb did an experiment with a cobra and a canary to find out. They barely had time to save the canary!

HOWEVER, a year after the discovery of the tomb, Carter asked a friend to look after his canary. Had he bought a new one, or was the old one still alive after all?

The Rumors Grow

Newspapers love the curse story, and it grows and grows. People start remembering—or thinking they remember—signs that had foretold Carnarvon's doom. One of the most popular stories is about the curse that was supposedly found in the tomb. Some say it was written on a wall, others say it was on an object of some kind. In fact, no curse has been found on anything, but even sensible people believe they have seen it. One young anthropologist who was shown around by Carter recalls being struck by an inscription over the door that said: "Death to those who enter." But no such inscription exists.

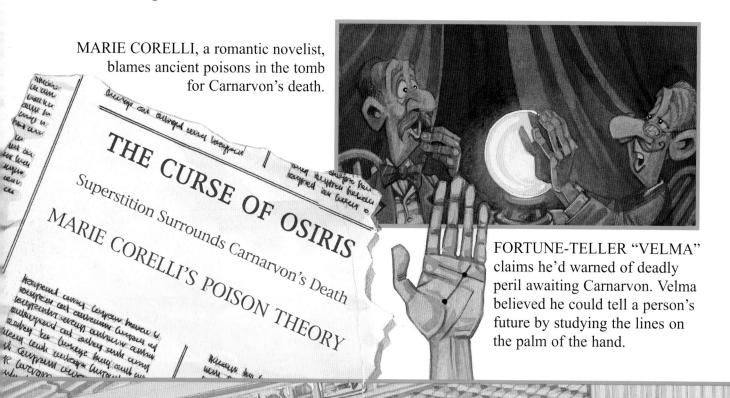

MARIE CORELLI, a romantic novelist, blames ancient poisons in the tomb for Carnarvon's death.

THE CURSE OF OSIRIS

Superstition Surrounds Carnarvon's Death

MARIE CORELLI'S POISON THEORY

FORTUNE-TELLER "VELMA" claims he'd warned of deadly peril awaiting Carnarvon. Velma believed he could tell a person's future by studying the lines on the palm of the hand.

THE BRITISH MUSEUM receives a flurry of packages containing statuettes and small pieces of mummies, sent by panicked collectors anxious to avoid a curse.

THE "MUMMY'S CURSE" has already been featured in books and films long before the Tutankhamen craze, but the rumors about his tomb give it a big boost.

The Death Toll Rises

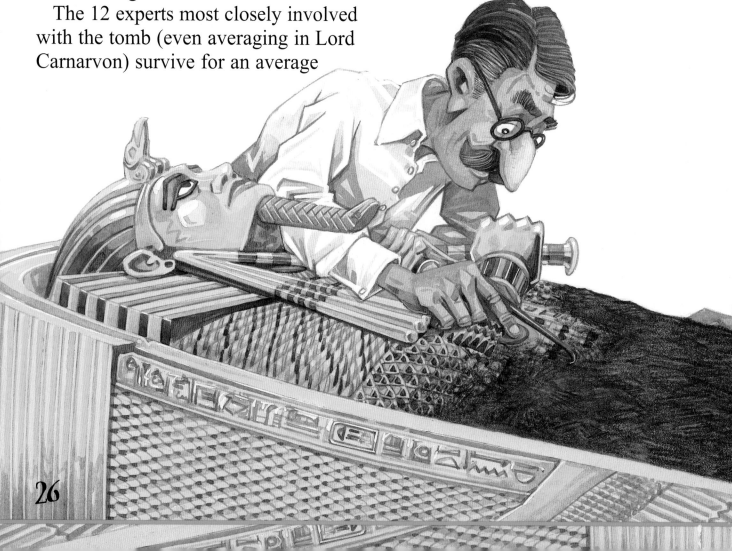

The curse of Tutankhamen makes such a good story that newspapers are eager to keep reporting on it. The death of anyone remotely connected with the tomb is written about in spooky terms to suggest that the curse is still at work. Yet the "curse" seems to miss some obvious targets.

The 12 experts most closely involved with the tomb (even averaging in Lord Carnarvon) survive for an average of 23 years (see page 31). Carnarvon's daughter, one of the first to enter the tomb, lives until 1980. Howard Carter should be the prime candidate for the curse, since he spends long hours working on Tutankhamen's coffins. The coffins are stuck together with hardened resin and Carter painstakingly chips it off. Yet he lives until 1939.

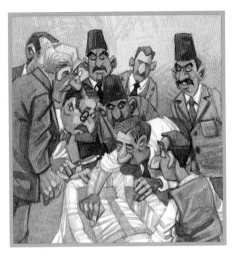

THE PEOPLE who were there as the mummy was actually unwrapped were all still alive nine years later.

Handy Hint

Don't believe everything you read in the papers.

More Victims?

THE DIRECTOR of Antiquities at the Louvre Museum in Paris, France, collapsed of heatstroke at the tomb and died. BUT he was 69.

ARTHUR MACE, one of Carter's assistants, died in 1928. BUT he had been suffering from heart, chest, and lung problems.

EGYPTIAN PRINCE Ali Fahmy Bey was shot by his wife in a hotel in London, England, soon after visiting the tomb. Whatever her reasons were, the curse was blamed.

IN 1929 a very unlucky chain of events made "curse" headlines. Carter's secretary died in London, of heart failure. The secretary's elderly father, overcome by the news, fell from a seventh-floor window. Later, his funeral hearse ran over a small boy on the way to the cemetery. If that was Tutankhamen's vengeance, it seems extreme!

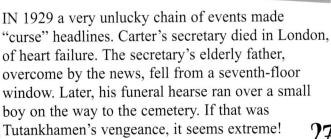

The Real Victim

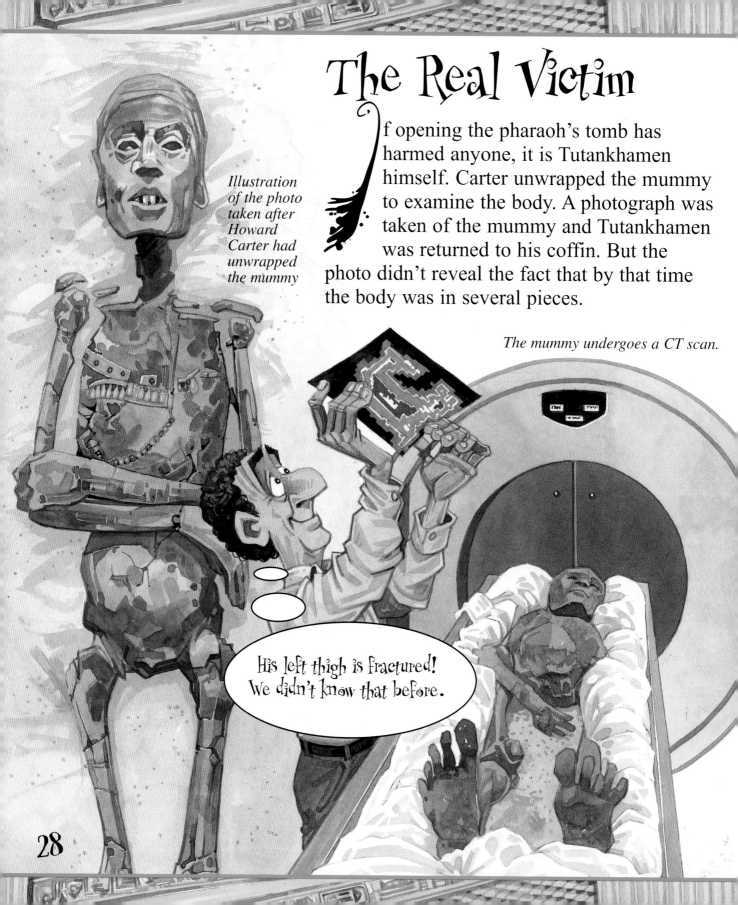

Illustration of the photo taken after Howard Carter had unwrapped the mummy

If opening the pharaoh's tomb has harmed anyone, it is Tutankhamen himself. Carter unwrapped the mummy to examine the body. A photograph was taken of the mummy and Tutankhamen was returned to his coffin. But the photo didn't reveal the fact that by that time the body was in several pieces.

The mummy undergoes a CT scan.

His left thigh is fractured! We didn't know that before.

The true damage to the body was revealed in 1968 when the mummy was removed from the coffin again and X-rayed. Carter had not been able to get the body out of the coffin whole because of hardened resin around it, so he had removed it in pieces. More bits of the mummy broke off when it was disturbed for another X-ray in 1978 and then for a CT scan in 2005. What a tragic fate for an ancient Egyptian, who believed that without a complete body his spirit would die!

Handy Hint

There may be real hazards in tombs rather than curses. Archeologists now wear masks to protect against microorganisms.

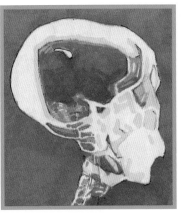

THE 1968 X-RAY showed a chip of bone inside the king's skull. This at first suggested he'd had a head injury, but now it is thought that Howard Carter may have done the damage.

THE X-RAY of Tutankhamen in 1968 revealed that his breastbone and part of his rib cage were missing.

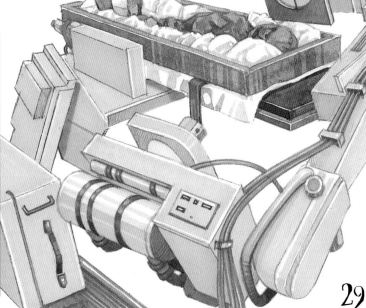

A 1978 PHOTO showed more damage. The eye sockets had sunk, the eyelids were gone, and the right ear was missing.

Glossary

Anthropologist A person who studies and compares human societies and cultures.

Archeologist A person who studies the remains of past civilizations.

Belzoni, Giovanni (1778–1823) An Italian hired by an English collector to hunt for Egyptian antiquities. He had an amazing knack for finding tombs. Although basically a treasure hunter, he helped lay the foundation for the modern science of Egyptology.

Blood poisoning A condition in which harmful bacteria from an infection invade the bloodstream, causing very high fever.

Carnarvon, George Herbert, **5th Earl of** (1866–1923) A wealthy Englishman who began excavating in Egypt to pass the time. He became hooked, even though in his first year all he found was a mummified cat. Realizing he didn't really know where to dig, he decided to hire a specialist: Howard Carter.

Carter, Howard (1874–1939) An archeologist who had no university training. He came to Egypt at the age of 17 as a draftsman and learned on the job. He was a careful and conscientious worker, devoting the rest of his life to studying the tomb of Tutankhamen and its contents.

CT scan A type of X-ray that produces a three-dimensional image. *CT* stands for "computed tomography."

Embalmer A person who preserves bodies from decay.

Hieroglyphs Signs representing words, syllables, or sounds that formed the ancient Egyptian alphabet.

Immortality The ability to live forever.

Jackal An animal of the dog family, found in Asia and Africa.

Microorganisms Living things invisible to the naked eye, such as bacteria and mold spores.

Nile The very long river that flows northward through Egypt.

Omen An object or event that is regarded as a sign of future disaster.

Resin A sticky substance obtained from trees.

Ritual tools Tools used in a religious ceremony.

Sarcophagus A chest-shaped coffin made of stone that may have one or more smaller coffins inside it.

Scarab A dung beetle. Scarabs roll balls of dung along the ground, and for the ancient Egyptians this was a symbol of the sun god rolling the sun across the sky.

Seal A piece of soft wax, plaster, or other material with an individual design stamped into it. It is attached to a door, letter, or container to secure it and prove that its contents have not been tampered with.

Shrine A container enclosing a sacred object.

Shroud A sheetlike wrapping for a corpse.

Telegram A message sent by telegraph.

Telegraph office A place for sending long-distance messages instantly along a wire, from an electric transmitter to a receiver that printed them out.

Tutankhamen A pharaoh of the 18th dynasty (family of rulers), who ruled Egypt from 1333 to 1323 BC.

Note: The 12 experts most closely involved with the tomb of Tutankhamen (see page 26) were: Howard Carter, Lord Carnarvon, Arthur Callender, Arthur Mace, Alfred Lucas, Harry Burton, Percy Newberry, James Breasted, Alan Gardiner, Douglas Derry, Lindsley Foote Hall, and Walter Hauser.

Index

A
amulets 8, 9
Anubis 8, 12

B
Belzoni, Giovanni 16
Bey, Ali Fahmy 27
blood poisoning 21
British Museum, London 25

C
Cairo Museum 18
Callender, Arthur 16
canary 22–23
Carnarvon, Lord 5, 16–17, 18,
  20–21, 24, 26
Carter, Howard 5, 16, 18, 19,
  22, 24, 26, 28–29
cobra 22–23
coffins 5, 9, 10, 26, 28
Corelli, Marie 24
CT scan 29
curse 14, 20, 24–25, 26–27

D
dog, death of 21

E
electricity failure 21
embalming 8–9

F
funeral 10–11

G
gods 6, 8
grave goods 11, 12

H
hieroglyphs 14
hunting 7

J
jewelry 9, 11, 14

L
Louvre Museum, Paris 27

M
Mace, Arthur 27
microorganisms 29
mosquito 20–21
mummy, mummification
  8–9, 12, 27, 28–29

N
newspapers, newspaper
  reporters 5, 18–19, 20, 24, 26
Nile 10, 11

O
omens 20
Opening of the Mouth 11

P
pneumonia 21
priests 7, 8, 10, 12, 20

R
Ra, ancient Egyptian sun
  god 8
robbers, robberies 14–15

S
sarcophagus 12
scarab 8
seals, sealing 12, 14
shrines 12
survival rates 26

T
tomb
  excavating 16–17, 18–19
  robbing 14–15
  sealing 12–13

V
Valley of the Kings 10, 11,
  16–17
"Velma" 24

W
Weigall, Arthur 19, 22

X
X-rays 29

Adapted from *King Tut's Curse!*, first published in Great Britain in 2006 © The Salariya Book Co. Ltd.